Sage

Homeschooling

A lifestyle for a connected family

Rachel Rainbolt, M.A.

Author: Rachel Rainbolt, M.A.
Editor: Casey Ebert, M.F.A
Designer: Joshua Rainbolt, M.F.A.

Disclaimer:
I recommend that parents consider options and become
as informed as is possible, matching what you learn with
what you think can work the best for you, your child, and
your family. You must use your wisdom and discretion
in deciding what is in the best interest of your child.
The material in this book is meant to be considered in
this process, providing perspective, anecdotes, tools,
techniques and information for your inspiration and
consideration. The products and product considerations
recommended in this book are personal preferences.
You are encouraged to investigate and form your own
opinions as to the rightness of fit of any product for
you and your child. The information in this book is not
meant to be considered medical or psychotherapeutic
advice. Rachel Rainbolt, Sage Parenting, is not liable or
responsible for the parenting or educational choices you
make, actions you take, or any consequences thereof.

ISBN:-10: 1494953919
ISBN-13: 978-1494953911

Dedication

Kai, thank you for showing me what you need, for your passion, and for bravely soaring.

Bay, thank you for confidently forging your own path, for harnessing your unique strengths, and for flourishing.

West, thank you for blazing down your trail, holding my hand, with a grin and a smart sense of adventure.

Joshua, thank you for having enough faith in me to take the leap and for making this life possible by being who you are and doing all you do.

Daddy, thank you for always being there for us. Your support is a key ingredient to my family's success.

Mom, thank you for being encouraging of our decision to homeschool.

Emily, thank you for being *my* homeschooling guide.

Contents

1

Following the Footpath

Busy school drop-offs, awkward school pictures, playground politics, and stacks of worksheets were all staples of my childhood. My school-based universe not only occupied my days, but also shaped the lens through which I was to view the world and defined my place in it. School constructed the box into which we were all to fit and set us in our place on the American assembly line.

Most never question this reality as a staple of life any more than they would question eating turkey on Thanksgiving. Education is a cornerstone of our society. Schools are the factories that churn out "Americans." As such, traditional schools are beyond reproach. What would my childhood have been like without school? It wouldn't have existed (said with righteous indignation). My childhood was school. It was the sun (er, black hole?) in my universe in that it was the force around which my life and very personhood orbited, determining the habitability of my atmosphere. To be clear, I didn't dislike school, per se. I did well. Like a fish in a fish tank, I just didn't know there was an ocean.

So naturally, not only did I not question that my children would go to traditional school (Even prefacing the word school with "traditional" betrays my enlightenment. Sorry, it's just school.), I didn't even know there was any other option (unless you were part of a proselytizing religious cult, allergic to the poisonous hocus-pocus of science and opting instead for gospel in the church basement with your faith healer, or a 1%er sending your prince to Sir Douchebag Academy).

As my Sunshine's launch into this celebrated milestone loomed, I became queasy over the shady details of this arrangement I seemed to have already signed off on when I filled out his birth certificate. I thought, is the world crazy? I'm supposed to hand over my little 4-year-old to a complete stranger surrounded by a wild pack of rabid hooligans for six hours of every day?! Are you insane?! This small person, into whom I have poured my best intentions and efforts for every minute of the last four years, is now going to be stamped with a barcode and ripped into the current of "He'll survive." I'm sorry, but my standards are higher than mere survival (and frankly, with the climate of bullying, not everyone does survive a public school adolescence). I want to help him thrive. How can one teacher possibly feed the passionate fire of curiosity of 30 kindergarteners in a way that respects each individual learning style and contextualizes the knowledge in the real world? But alas, I must be the crazy one. After all, everyone does it (Red flag! Anytime you are using that logic to convince yourself something is a good choice, take a step back and reevaluate!), so I'm sure it will be fine, and it is what's in his best interest.

I resided in the best district, I interviewed principals, and I carefully researched (any limited) options. He was a smart, sweet boy, with a snappy first day of school outfit, who could already read. And while he was a champ, the experience was a nightmare. Turns out, all of my concerns were valid, and just because most people do something doesn't mean it's in your best interest (duh).

The teacher was miserable (she had a palpable disdain for the children and her job). The school program was institutional and completely missed the mark of my son's best interest (rigorous and frequent testing was the foundation of the learning program, 45 minutes of silent, seated writing was not developmentally appropriate for kindergarten, and college readiness in the form of weekly hour-long, college-pep assemblies on the hot blacktop were considered the core learning motivators). The socialization was not how I would want my child socialized (he was even bullied with, "I have a gun at my house and I know how to shoot people," by a fellow 5-year-old).

The phrase I heard more than any other during our year at this school was, "We want independent learners." That was their party line, recited when a student had a question, needed help, tried to discuss something with another student, requested attention of any kind, or generally stuck out of the stifling mold. My response: "I send him here for cooperative group learning. We could independently learn at home."

While homeschool lingered in the back of my mind, I dismissed its legitimacy out of hand with platitudes such as, "He's so social," and "I don't want to be a teacher." I desperately concluded that it must be the school. So we changed schools.

The truth is, I wasn't brave enough. That is the bottom line, hard truth, that I have to live with. I wasn't brave enough to walk away from something so ingrained... yet.

First grade was eons better than our kindergarten experience. His teacher was fantastic and he loved her. The school was "high quality," and the families held the school accountable for the best experience traditional public school could offer. But the raging fire in my son, which once burned with a passion for learning, was dying. The spark of individuality and leadership that could yield a real world-changer was being snuffed out. He had friends and did well academically. But he was not happy, and school was not fostering his best self. There was no room for joy in traditional school.

Halfway through the second grade school year, we had had our fill with the teacher, the kind of socialization the school was providing, and the system at large. This moment provided just the catalyst we needed to jump ship. I was scared, and I didn't know much of anything about homeschooling, but I was ready to take on that fear and uncertainty for my son.

2

Stepping onto a New Path

I found the perfect option for our situation: the homeschool program through our school district. Since it was the middle of the school year, I was able to simply collect all of my son Skyler (Kai's) books and seamlessly transfer over to doing the exact same work, but only meeting with a homeschool teacher once a week to turn in our workload and get the next week's assignments. It was perfect at the time because a big fear of ours with homeschooling was that he could fall academically behind. This course of action meant that he would maintain his academic position, completing the same work at pace with his former peers. Plus, if we found it to be a disastrous choice, we could effortlessly return to traditional schooling.

To call the first weeks of homeschooling through our district eye opening would be a gross understatement. I was shocked. I felt like a fool. I felt betrayed. I had been loyal to a system with which I had entrusted my progeny. I knew the costs of traditional education but assumed they were worth it. I assumed the gain I wasn't directly seeing was immense. I was wrong. Upon looking behind the curtain, there was no wizard. There were several things that I was immediately struck by and spent the first weeks reeling over.

First, I was flabbergasted by the minute amount of work my son was actually doing in school. Now, we went to a great public school, in one of the best districts in our state (as determined by test scores). The teachers were of the highest quality. But what you don't realize from your parent seat outside the school gates is that most of the day is spent on classroom management. With one teacher and 30-something little kids, the bulk of time and energy is expended on things like turning in papers, cleaning up, lining up, settling down, gathering here and there, commanding attention, etc. My son, who likes to take his time, completed the entire workload for a week of traditional schooling (reminder: we are talking about literally the exact same work) in three days, working only three hours a day. My immediate knee-jerk reaction was, what the hell are they doing the rest of the time? He had to be incarcerated for 30 hours a week to complete nine hours of work?

Second, I was disappointed to discover that the vast majority of the work he was doing was completely menial. It was busywork. It was work that would require hours of silent plug and chug with no higher thinking or meaningful learning. I get it. I get that that is how it makes sense to disperse assignments in a room full of students with only one teacher. It would yield a quiet room with moving pencils. Circle the verb. Color the bat. Add the numbers. But it is an incredibly inefficient avenue for learning.

Third, I was genuinely surprised to find that they progress so slowly. I suppose this makes sense given that they do so little, and it's mostly mere busywork. But it still stumped me for a while. It's as though the natural learning momentum is almost completely stalled in the practical grind of traditional school life. Student reads: Abraham Lincoln passed this law. Student queries: Hey, how do we pass a law? Teacher responds: Stop talking, copy the fact, and color in his hat. We have five more minutes before computer lab."

Fourth, I was blown away by just how much was accomplished for my son's education with only one weekly teacher meeting, which never even lasted more than 30 minutes. For example, his district homeschool teacher once asked, "Are there any things you think we should look at?"

"Well, his teachers have always complained about his handwriting. I could not care less. Neatness of handwriting has never been an area in which he exceled, and quite frankly, I don't have any concerns about him being 25 and not being able to communicate effectively in writing. Maybe he'll grow up to be a doctor."

"Write your name on this piece of paper," she told my son. He took the pencil and wrote his name. "He holds his pencil wrong and presses too hard. Frequently, when kids get in the habit of holding their pencil incorrectly, their handwriting appears sloppy, and when they press too hard, their hands cramp and they fatigue out – they can't get through as many worksheets at their desks on their own. Have his teachers ever complained of that? Let's put this special thing on your pencil." She taught him how to use it. "Now try to write your name and press lightly." His handwriting was instantly 10 times better.

OMFG! "His teachers have been complaining about those two very things for years. All the hours of time they spent telling him he was bad at handwriting and needed to 'do better'; all those times I replied with 'Do you have any suggestions?' and was told, 'Have him write more for longer'; and all those times they whined that when he is expected to sit at his desk for long periods of time writing on his own, he looses focus and stops writing, they could have just spent 60 seconds watching him write one word and fixed the problem (which was really their problem, as he and I didn't really care that much other than to get the teachers off his back about it)?!"

Mind. Blown. Even using the same basic curriculum as our school district, with a school district teacher, the structure of homeschool instantly freed us to see and do exactly what was best for him. It took a one-on-one teacher 60 seconds to do what years of traditional schooling couldn't do! The amount of time teachers dedicated to whining about that issue was an absurd and utter waste that could have been remedied with one minute of personalized education.

Fifth, without the limits of a one-size-fits-all curriculum for 30-40 unique learners, the teacher and I were able to tailor curricula for my child's specific needs. This freedom of options was empowering and effective. For example, during our second meeting with our district teacher, she sat down at a table with us, flipped through the work we turned in, asked my son some questions about some of the concepts he was supposed to learn, and turned to me saying, "He is right where he should be, but he is bored and easily understands all of the concepts. What seems to hold him back in the curriculum?"

"He hates the busywork. Anytime he is actually learning new concepts, he loves and moves through the work quickly."

"That's what I see also. You know, there is another math

curriculum that you should look into that moves through the concepts more quickly and cuts out a lot of the repetition and practice he doesn't need or want. You can look into it, and come back next week and let me know if you want to switch to that, and I'll help you map it out. Let's tweak things for sure so he gets what he needs/wants. Let's get these things out of his way so he can move at *his* pace."

After surprisingly little time out of the full-time system (without The Man holding him down), my Sunshine came alive! His light once again shone brightly! His powerful drive for deep, inquisitive conversation, which had all but disappeared under the weight of three years of traditional public schooling, quickly reemerged. An endless stream of questions and insistent discussion again sounded between us like my favorite song playing on the radio. His eagerness to know and understand more again overtook his now freed resources of time, focus, and energy. The pressures of fitting into the mold now melted away, and his heavy posture gave way to floating and bouncing with every step. With the duct tape peeled off, the shackles broken and the veil of repression lifted, he was free to soar – and soar he did.

Critical thinking, *creativity*, and *curiosity* were reintegrated into his life (just as Sir Ken Robinson would have predicted based on his superb talk *How Schools Kill Creativity*[1], which happens to be the most popular TED Talk of all time)! They just sprouted out of him like a deeply rooted redwood that reconnected with its water source. He once again embraced learning in every moment and environment. Finally, I thought, this is the way it should be. It feels so right! The repression of his average traditional school experience is gone. *He just has such **profound happiness.***

The hours of busywork gave way to natural learning in a self-driven form that was meaningful and lasting. Writing an arbitrary list of random vocabulary words over and over was ditched. When I read to him every night, he stopped me at every word he didn't know, and we had a whole discussion around deciphering its meaning. His vocabulary was so much more enhanced through this organic, spontaneous inquisition than a stupid weekly spelling test.

While driving home from the Botanic Garden one day, he queried, "How are toes advantageous?" I explained, and he followed up with, "What is the name for the toe bones?"

"Phalanges, which connect to the metatarsals."

"Can we play Guess Who?!"

"Sure!"

"Okay, okay, I am a bone. I am circular. I am on the lower half of the body. I help your leg to bend."

"Oh, oh, the kneecap?"

"Yes! What is the name for the kneecap?"

"The patella."

"I am Mr. Patella!"

The game continued, as we took turns until we arrived at dinner. Once dessert arrived, he steered the evolution of his game to geography.
"I am a state. I am a series of islands. I was formed from a volcano, which is pretty cool. Daddy was born here!"

Bailey (Bay), my 5-year-old, yelled out, "Hawaii!" and he took his own turn. "I am to the right. I am an island. I am full of lost people. I am Neverland!" (He is Peter Pan obsessed.) Then, after a hearty laugh, I suggested he try again with Antarctica, for which he was able to give some great clues.

As another example, upon finishing the *Peter and the Starcatchers* book we were reading, Kai exclaimed that he wanted to tell everyone how awesome the book was so they would know to read it too. I told him I would be happy to post a book review on my blog for all the families who follow my work to read. We did a little research and found that a helpful book review contains a brief summary, followed by a written opinion, and he was off. His enthusiasm sparkled with every keystroke of that review, which he wrote all on his own and proudly emailed the link to our family and his friends.

This is just a window into the new way, or really a reversion to the way it was before traditional school squelched it, we learn. It feels like nothing is crammed down his throat anymore, so he is no longer in a constant state of choking down vegetables. He is free to eat according to his own hunger, and his appetite for learning is insatiable! And I get to encourage and provide a means to satisfy that hunger and be a fun partner on the ride.

After spending hours doing worksheets through our district curriculum, we went to the Blue Sky Nature Preserve across the street for a nature hike. My son left his science test (Forms of Matter) for some real world learning. As we walked through the trail surrounded by trees that were recovering after a major fire years earlier (and talked all about the role of fires in the ecosystem), a lizard caught his eye. Right in front of us was a blackened tree, and he was staring at a barely visible lizard, next to two other lizards, on the trunk.

> "Wow, you can barely even see that lizard on that tree. Do you remember what one of the lizard's super survival strategies is?"

> "Blending in! Camouflage!"

"That's right! Now what color are the lizards we usually see?"

"Brown."

"Yeah. And what color are this lizard and his friends?"

"Blackish."

"Yes, they are. I also see that the lightest one is missing his tail."

"Yeah, that is another one of their super survival strategies – it grows back!"

"That's right. Now what do you think would happen if a light brown lizard was hanging out here on these trees?"

"What do you mean?"

"Well, would he blend in, or would a predator spot him and make him lunch?"

"You would see him."

"Yup. So here in Blue Sky, since all these trees were blackened in the fire, the blackish lizards survive and make black baby lizards, while more light brown lizards get eaten. The black lizards are *selected for*. That is called **Natural Selection**. That is evolution: How species *evolve* over time based on what they need to survive in their environment. Now what do you think will happen over the years as these trees regrow their natural brown bark?"

"Then the blackish lizards will get eaten more, and there will be more brown lizards. Are the brown lizards extinct right now?"

"No, they aren't extinct, but there aren't as many
of them."

He then went on about how sad it was that some of the
lizards died. "What if it was a Mommy lizard?" After Bay
named the lizard – "Blacky!" –we went on our way. This
will stay with him. This was real life. This experience
allowed him to take a complex concept like evolution or
natural selection or forest fires or animal adaptations
and, in one hour-long walk, apply all that knowledge in
meaningful and lasting ways. Meanwhile, his peers were
sitting in a classroom filling out more worksheets and
taking more tests.

By the end of the school year, we were ecstatic and
our lives were transformed. It felt as though we
reverted to a natural state where everything that
had come between us, everything that had disrupted
our happiness, our harmony, and our journey of self-
actualization, was now gone. We were sold. We were
not going back. The only negativity or conflict now in my
heart was the regret of not choosing this path from the
beginning, when my intuition knew best.

3

View from the
Other Side

So, to empower you to make an informed decision for your child's educational journey, I am going to address some of what initially held me back from homeschooling, from my vantage point now on the other side.

"I don't want to be a teacher."
In homeschooling my child I am no more or less a teacher than I have been every day to him for the seven years before making this change. I am his ambassador to the universe. *That* is the flip in the mindset of homeschooling that makes it so amazing! My error in thinking was that in homeschooling I would have to change myself and/or my relationship with my

children to fit the teacher-student/classroom model. But that is all wrong. We get to continue our parent-child relationship, accentuating my guiding role in support of his leadership on his journey. I am not stepping into the role of his classroom teacher. We are expanding our parent-child/mentor-mentee relationship.

"My kid doesn't like learning from me."
Wrong. My kid loves learning from me. I am his archetype for what it means to learn. From the moment he was placed on my chest after birth, he learned love, trust, and security, and we have continued in that vein every day since. What he didn't like was having me be the warden of his extended prison sentence of hours of homework time. And that, as I have now learned, is not what school has to be like. It most certainly is not what learning looks like. Now when he learns through me, he takes my hand.

"I want a career."
Six hours a day in school (sitting at a desk, pounding out work) plus three hours of mindless busywork, I mean homework, every day. At 7 years old. He meets his curriculum objectives in homeschool in a fraction of this time. He learns faster, moves through things quicker, and is *happier*. So what does all this mean for a career? It means I am spending less time homeschooling than I did traditional schooling. You read that right. Between get up and ready, drop-off, back home, pick-up, after school checklist, homework, misery, rebellion, (Okay, he was always a good kid, and I might be being a bit dramatic here, but his unhappiness from the school environment did suck up time and attention.), etc., my time was always harried. Now we spend a couple hours cuddled on the couch during my baby's naptime (on my chest) going through something together, and he works a little on his own (usually first thing in the morning).

I own and operate my own company. I did when he was in public school. I do now that we homeschool. There is a next step in my career that I look forward to taking. I had planned to work during the hours my kids were in school, once my youngest was in kindergarten, to take that next step. But I can easily homeschool my children in the mornings and work in the afternoons or vice versa, or homeschool three days a week and work two full days, etc. There is so much flexibility and possibility. I have been so pleasantly surprised by this. My husband suggested that once I am ready to make that step, we could hire a tutor of sorts to come in to help, but I would prefer some help in the form of a weekly housekeeper or something of that nature instead. Help with another of my less important jobs would be appreciated in moving forward in my career. But I am so happy to report feeling that homeschooling and advancing my career are harmoniously integrated.

"I asked my child, and he doesn't want to homeschool." Asking children who have only ever been in traditional school if they want to homeschool is like asking children if they want to give up their current diet in favor of food they have never before eaten. Traditional school is the only life they know. Not many children would immediately give up the devil they know. I believe the opinions and viewpoints of our children should weigh heavily on our decision-making. I also believe that there are times in life when we can see a broader view and have to make a decision for them that we believe to be in their best interest. Ideally, this decision would be collaborative; you could thoroughly investigate together by discussing goals and concerns, priorities and options.

"It's extremist."
Okay, I too needed to push those images of fundamentalist Christians with dozens of children out of my mind. I am not homeschooling to shelter my children from the blasphemous teachings of Satan's science. And I don't ever concern myself with judgments. I think what I was really thinking was, *I will be all alone in this.* But as I

have opened up my journey to others, particularly in my supportive circle (mama tribe), I have been so affirmed and encouraged by their overwhelming support. I am not alone. I needed only to reach out a hand, and I have been connected with others just like me and other kids like mine. I am not alone in this, and neither are you.

"I can't do it with younger siblings under wing."
I have three little boys who are now 8, 5, and Weston (West) is 2. The totally awesome phenomenon in which I am currently reveling is that my older child teaches his younger brother all the cool stuff he learns! This takes his understanding of the concepts to a whole different level, and his younger brother learns all kinds of things that had never even crossed his radar. It trickles on down the line and sometimes even up. Just last night my bigger boys were in the backseat of the car spontaneously quizzing each other with addition problems. They were practicing math, encouraging each other, and having fun.

"I believe in the value to society of public education. I don't see homeschool as the answer to the fundamental problems of the way we teach children in the public school system."
This is still true. But I can no longer sacrifice my child's well-being for the sake of campaigning for systemic change that is far, far off. I have to do what is in the best interest of my child and my family. And right now, that is homeschooling.

"He is so social; he would not like homeschooling."
My child is so very social. He loves interacting with others and so treasures his friendships. But even he reached a point when he knew it wasn't worth it. He had quality friendships that would and have carried over. And we are integrating all kinds of social activities into his life to strengthen those social networks outside of school. For example, did you know that even if you are homeschooling you still have access to all of the auxiliary

programs through the public school? For example, my son had the solo in his elementary school choir. He could still do choir! Plus, we have since embarked on a learning path through a homeschool charter where my kids attend a learning center class with a peer group two days a week (and love it). Even outside of these institutions there is *ample* opportunity for creating a strong social network. Any activity offered within school is also offered outside of school. Combine that with homeschool Meetup groups, playdates, and the myriad children's organizations in existence, and your social plate can be plenty full.

"I don't want to homeschool forever."
I don't need to decide what is in the best interest of my 14-year-old child today while he is 5. Today I must decide what is in the best interest of my 5-year-old. And what is in the best interest of my 5-year-old is homeschool. We always have the option of reentering public school at any moment – literally, any day. We also have a number of other options in between.

"My child won't be on par with his peers."
Not only is he on par with his peers, but also this amazing thing happened where, in making this switch, he is able to accelerate beyond what he was capable of before while in the confines of the school machine. Plus, he is able to learn what suits his brain now and able to tackle things in the way that works best for him. For example, I was able to find a language arts curriculum that taps into his strengths and interests, which happens to be a curriculum for gifted students, and he finished the entire language arts program for third grade within the first two months of the school year. Unfortunately, he inherited my lack of affection for math, so out of concern for it being completed, I requested that one of his three daily subjects be his main math curriculum until it was done. He finished the book halfway through the semester and now doesn't have to worry about it. It's now easy for me to see how so many homeschool

children earn a high school diploma in their early teen
years.

In addition to learning all of these concepts, he gains
ownership of his learning, freedom to grow into his
unique self, and joy. So will he be on par with his peers?
No. He will be an even more well-rounded person.

This example illustrates yet another great lesson of
homeschooling: there is no one optimal timeline for a
child's learning. It's not a competition, and it's not a race.
The freedom to follow my child's unique learning journey
without the pressure of some arbitrary timeline has been
stress relieving and confidence boosting to say the least.

"I'm not _____ enough."
You are. Whatever it is, you are. There's this amazing
aspect of parenthood: We have within us the potential
to rise to the occasion. It might require some work or
tapping into some resources, but whatever it is that
causes you to doubt yourself today, you are enough.

Think about what holds you back, and challenge it.

On the Right Path

So after finding the courage to make the initial jump, we now had a whole semester of heavily structured homeschooling, under the direct supervision of our home district, under our belts and a very successfully educated child to show for it. With that came the confidence to dive into the foreign world of homeschooling. I devoured every book on the subject. I read every article I could track down. I connected myself with friends of friends and social media groups to tap into the resources, support, and wisdom of others in our community of homeschoolers. I discovered a whole world of research-supported, scientifically sound information and educated, well-socialized, fun people. Through this research, I uncovered countless options at my disposal for educating our children.

If your local school district has a homeschool program (usually started for a bedridden student with a medical condition or a child actor with a pressing commercial schedule (or maybe that's just here in Southern California)), it can provide a lot of traditional resources and structure for an uncertain rookie homeschooler. You'll have strict standards keeping you in line, which is restricting yet comforting in the early days of straying from the flock of the mainstream. The upside is that you also have access to all of the auxiliary aspects of traditional schooling, such as band, choir, and PE (Physical Education), plus a full spectrum of any special services your child might need without the hefty expense. The downside is definitely that you are still very much in the traditional school system, which means lots of busywork and a limiting core curriculum. You are still not the director of your child's learning and answer to someone else who lives within the confines of the big system.

At the opposite end of the homeschooling spectrum, you do have the freedom to go completely solo. In most states, you register yourself as a school (seems bizarre, I know) and you can be totally off the grid. This option would be perfect for the child with the French model mother who travels frequently for long photo shoots or the child who farms on an unplugged commune. Okay, I'm obviously being facetious, but you get the point. The upside to total freedom is that you don't have to answer to anyone. The downside is that you don't have any support, either. If this feels like a good fit for you, search on your state's website and you can usually find the form you need to fill out. Then voila! You're off the grid.

In today's world, you need only hop on the computer to go to school. There are many reputable online charter schools that can meet your standard school needs. The upside is that they are all-in-one (everything you need to be comprehensively underway is provided) and require less of the parent. The downside is that all-in-one means no flexibility, and fewer parental requirements means less parental involvement, both of which are part of what I love about homeschooling.

Perhaps traditional schooling is not right for your family, but you are not ready to turn your back on full-time schooling. There is a great big world of charter schools out there, at the forefront of pedagogic research (not limited and restrained by the bureaucracy of the public education system), tailored to specific interests or styles. In my city of San Diego there are so many charter schools that, before I took the plunge and left the traditional school system, I didn't even know existed. A simple Google search could yield a wealth of options that were not even on your radar. For example, there is a great charter in my neighborhood that is a fully state-funded, four-day Montessori education program.

The ideal option for us – where we have truly found a perfect fit – is with a local homeschool charter[2]. For our school, we meet with a teacher once a month just to check in, we homeschool on our own, and my children attend a learning center class two days a week.

We initially met with our EF (Educational Facilitator) in the resource library, which houses all of the curricula. There we discussed my children's individual learning styles (I now had a third-grader and kindergartener) and planned out which curricula and supplies we wanted to meet my children's educational needs. Each child is allotted a certain number of EUs (Educational Units), or dollars, given by the state to the school, to be used for the child's education. We checked out what was readily available. We ordered "consumables" (items like workbooks that are only used once). And we signed the boys up for the learning center classes.

The learning center classes that my boys attend are in a program that is project-based (which has a lot of great new research support), child-led, and free of the responsibility of teaching a state-mandated curriculum (as the homeschooling done with the parent provides the primary education). Bay is in a K/1 class (with about six kids), and Kai is in a 2/3 class (with about eight), though in my observation, the two classes are frequently together. These classes allow them two days a week in a different environment with a regular peer group and another adult who guides their learning. They get a little bit of separateness but are still connected. They *love* these classes. I wake them up on these two mornings and they grin from ear to ear, happily chatting away about all the fun they will have that day.

I think part of why they thrive with this arrangement is the balance. Monday they wake up early and have their exciting learning center experience. Tuesday they rise on their own, well-rested, and leisurely work on their workbooks in the hammock in the backyard, followed by a playdate at a museum. The next day we might take a nature hike followed by swim practice. We have the perfect balance for us and the freedom to tweak things to maintain that optimal balance for each child.

Basically, the learning center serves the function of facilitating big art-based group projects. Can you do big art-based group projects with straight homeschooling? Sure. Did I? Not really. Honestly, with a toddler also under wing, that was the only piece I felt could have been stronger for my eldest when we were homeschooling through the district. These classes are completely different from a traditional classroom, and I think the word that sums it up best is *respect.* This homeschool charter has respect for each individual child as a person and each individual learning journey.

Check out this video clip[3] from the film *Finding Joe*[4] by Patrick Takaya Solomon, which was shown to us at orientation for our homeschool charter, about discovering your child's inner golden nature through The Golden Buddha metaphor. It reflects the nature of the program we have found resonates with us.

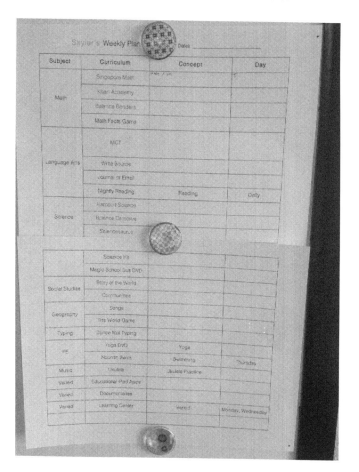

For the other three days of the school week, we homeschool. What that actually looks like varies greatly from family to family. For us, homeschooling is organized around a Weekly Plan I created for each of my children, which is a chart consisting of all of their subject/ curriculum options. It's a mix of modalities and subjects including various learning tools such as an anatomy app on the iPad to a literacy workbook, a chemistry lab set to a social studies textbook. Each homeschool day, they choose three items from the plan, and we fill in the chart with the topic they learned. When we meet with our EF for our monthly home-visit meeting, that is what we turn in. And each child has a shelf with all of his curricula for the year. We now answer only to our own personal learning journeys, which is fantastic.

We do not have a traditional-classroom-in-a-home-setting vibe by any means. You will never see me standing up at a blackboard while the three children sit at a desk. It is just our fun, cozy life with some extra required work and bonus quiet one-on-one instruction time. Bay and I read about magnetism in his science textbook. I pulled out our magnet box (magnet wands, discs, balls, and paperclips), a glass of water, and a cardboard box. They have excitedly created a magnet world around me, complete with ice-skating Spiderman. They have already requested a trip to the science museum tomorrow (which has hands-on magnetic science experiments). The lessons come to life with the curricula serving as a springboard.

Conquering the Terrain

The physical environment of your child's playscape is a
metaphor for your child's internal state. Are you setting
your child up for success with optimal playscape design?
Is your home environment conducive to learning?
Organization fosters calmness, while disorganization
fosters chaos. Appropriate toy storage paired with
an easily maintained system of organization is key.
An environment full of play opportunities from all the
developmental areas, across the zone of proximal
development, spurs self-directed learning through play.
It goes even beyond that in that you can tailor your
environment to the specific personality and needs of
your child, setting your little one up for success and

you up for easier days (e.g., closed toy storage, calming colors like blues, and classical music for a child who is easily overstimulated).

Children learn through play! In the immortal words of Fred Rogers, "Play is often talked about as if it were a relief from serious learning. But for children play is serious learning. Play is really the work of childhood." Play is the language of children. It is the playground for their minds, and toys are the tools of their development. In addition to having the structured opportunities for learning through curricula, our homeschool environment is brimming with opportunities for discovery and mental exercise through play. Here are some ways to create and maintain such a space.

Rotate Toys

To understand the value of this method you must first understand habituation. When something is in the same place for a long period of time, you no longer see it. It's like how you didn't even notice that hideous wallpaper in that apartment you rented after a few months. But each houseguest just had to remark, "Wow, that wallpaper just about knocks you over, doesn't it?" And you replied, "We're used to it now." This is habituation. Toys that are left in the same place for a long period of time (long being relative to a person who has only been alive for a few months or years) become wallpaper. When you rotate your toys, they become brand new with each rotation. The first step in harnessing the power of rotation is to have toys in a few places: downstairs living area, child's bedroom, and storage closet, for example. About every month, completely rotate out all of the toys. Take the toys from the storage closet and rotate them in. Move some toys from the living room to the bedroom and vice versa. The idea is to create a brand new play landscape for your little explorer.

Zone of Proximal Development

Your child's toys should reflect his zone of proximal development. This means that on your bookshelf of toys, there should be three categories of toys: those that are easily mastered by your child, those that are an active challenge but can be accomplished on his own with some effort, and those that are within his reach but he needs help to master. All three categories should be present in your child's toy world. This will provide his with confidence (the toys that are easily mastered), appropriate stimulation and challenge (the toys that present a significant challenge), and motivation for further growth (the toys that require help).

Organize

The organization process consists of three things: purge, sort, and store. The first step is to sort. Dump all your crap into a mountain and sit right in front of it. It's important not to become overwhelmed, as would be natural sitting in front of a mountain of crap. Take a deep breath and take it one thing at a time. Pick up the first item and put it in a pile. You will always have a trash pile. You will usually have a donate pile. The rest of the piles will vary depending upon what you are organizing. For example, when I sorted the art supplies, I had a big trash pile and then sorted the various supplies into piles like dry erase, chalk, erasers, stickers, etc.

Do not underestimate the importance of the purge. If you have not used something in the last year, get rid of it! Dried out markers – trash. That fast food toy they played with once – donate. Purging keeps your home, your sanctuary, relevant to your life today. If you do not purge, you will drown in clutter. Your children can be a part of this process too. Prior to any gift-giving holiday, have your kids go through their belongings and make a trash and donate pile to make room for the new presents they will receive.

Centers

Preschools have been hip to this concept for a while now, and the reason they use it is because it is good for the child and it works. Children play best when their play world is organized according to the aspect of brain development the play taps into. For example, one shelf on the bookshelf can be for puzzle-type toys, while a chest under the window can be for pretend play, containing all of the dress-up costumes. A fine motor center of art supplies is great next to their little table in the living room. Simply put, this is organization. But it can go a long way in helping to organize your children and help along play.

Sorting

Your toy storage must be set up in such a way that your child is able to clean up. If each toy is put away in its original packaging and filed on the top shelf, you are not only making your job more difficult (even if your child wanted to clean up, and most do, he couldn't) but you are denying your child the opportunity to develop growth in all the ways cleaning up provides. Cleaning up is a great left-brain growth activity because children must sort. All "guys" go in this box. All blocks go in that box. And of course, when you include your child in cleaning up, you are sending the message that he is an integral part of your family system; he has an important and valuable role. But to send this message, toys must be stored in such a way that your child can clean up. I use open-top, fabric-covered boxes on low shelves and closed, clear plastic latch boxes. When they want to play, they pull out the box. When it's time to clean up, we toss everything back in the box, and it is put back on the shelf. Each activity is contained and easily cleaned up.

Uniformity

Contrasting visual colors and patterns can be overstimulating. All of those visible toys and packaging with their loud patterns and colors can be stressful. Consider using toy storage that is uniform. Those open-top, fabric-covered boxes I mentioned above, they are all blue, green or wicker. This way, when you look at the toy areas, they are not visually overwhelming or stressful. Not to mention, it makes living spaces seem like child-integrated homes and not toy stores.

Labels

Labeling boxes and shelves is essential for staying organized. I love my lable maker, but prior to this lovely Christmas gift, I was simply printing titles, cutting them out, and taping them, or even writing on peel-and-stick labels. Labeled storage makes everything easy to find and clean up. Looking for your 2-inch Buzz Lightyear? Simply go to the "Guy" shelf and pull out the "Toy Story" box. It takes only seconds to locate a tiny toy among the hundreds of toys my three children are privileged to enjoy.

With a very young one, consider labeling your toys with a photo and word. If each activity is stored in a box, simply put a photo of what's inside along with the word on the front. Not only does this make organization easier (again, you want your child to be able to clean up) but it also teaches children pre-reading. They learn what the word "cars" looks like and, before long, recognize the word even without the picture. This is pre-reading.

Containers

So important! The importance of containers in organization cannot be understated. The proper container will function in such a way that independence and fascination will flourish. All that just from organized containers? Yes!

Just say no to original packaging. Original packaging takes up way more space than needed for the product contained within it (for more visible shelf space in the store), is visually loud (competing for your visual interest in the store), doesn't stay closed (pieces are always falling out and parts are always missing), is too difficult to open and close (your child can't take it out or clean it up), and is irregularly shaped (you can't efficiently stack it with other things from the same category).

I recommend a mixture of closed (you cannot see the toys inside the container) and open (the toys are on display within the container) toy storage. The bulk of the toys out and accessible in the room will be in closed toy storage to keep the space calm and relaxing. For this I love fabric, open-top boxes or woven, natural fiber boxes. Pick up a bunch and use them for bigger sets of toys such as cars, animals, pretend food, blocks, etc. These boxes look nice sitting on a bookshelf or in a cubed, cubby shelving system, are easily pulled off by a child for play with a particular activity, facilitate an easy clean up (simply toss toys back inside), and are easily placed back on the shelf. These can also effortlessly be rotated to keep the playscape fresh.

The final container that is essential to organization is what I refer to as the "latch box." The modular latch box is a system of small, clear boxes in varying sizes that all fit together.5 They are locked closed but can easily be opened with a latch by children. These latch boxes can sit on shelves, nested together, maximizing the usage of space, they can be used to store all of the toys that

are out of rotation, or they can be placed inside prettier
containers like the open-top fabric boxes. They allow me
to keep every toy we own organized. They are a perfect
excuse for chucking all that original packaging that
easily rips and falls open and the perfect solution for
keeping every single puzzle piece (simply cut out the
picture of the completed puzzle from the cardboard box
and enclose it in the latch box with the puzzle pieces),
game card, and small marble stored securely in its set. I
even use them for things like first-aid supplies (one box
for Tummy, Throat, Skin, etc.). My latch boxes are all
housed comfortably inside one bookshelf in the
playroom. I frequently pull down a box and feature it by
simply leaving it on the coffee table to take center stage
for my children's discovery and inevitable play.

Magnetic White Board: Displays our "weekly plan" or anything we want to feature.

Easy access area for my toddler's favorites or featured activities.

SageParenting.com

Feature

The open toy storage provides the opportunity to feature specific toys in the rotation. A container like shelved, tilted bins works well for this purpose. Right now I have one container full of various train sets, as my toddler is currently infatuated with trains (Thomas Trains in one bin, Geo Tracks in another, etc.), and one container full of sorted pretend food and dishes, right next to the pretend kitchen outside. Sometimes our feature bins will hold art supplies next to the easel or even facilitate scientific exploration with magnetic tools and toys. But as I mentioned above, even simply pulling down a random activity and leaving it out in an obvious place will rotate your children's attention to the variety of playthings they have at their disposal in their playscape.

Clean Up

By the age of 1, children can clean up with you. The
value and importance of cleaning up was discussed
earlier, but I want to emphasize that cleaning up should
be fun. If you approach it with disdain, like a chore,
then your child will do the same. Try singing a cleanup
song, giving lots of attention during cleanup time (eye
contact, physical touch, undivided attention), and have
fun! We literally toss each ball back into the box. It's like
basketball. We "zoom" each car into the box while it lies
sideways. As your child gets older, you can set a timer
and see how many toys he can pick up in 30 seconds.
When your child is a baby, it is much easier to clean
up the toys yourself. Involving your 12-month-old takes
much longer and requires more effort. But if you invest
the time and energy while young, your child will be
cleaning up on his own down the road.

Once your child is school-aged, clean up falls into two
categories of responsibility: personal and family. As an
individual family member, your child is responsible for
cleaning up after himself. Your child takes an activity
off the shelf, engages with it, and then puts it away. I
do not allow my children to move from mess to mess.
Once an activity is completed, it must be cleaned up
before a new activity may begin. This is not to say that
superheroes can't battle on the block tower, but before
you can go outside and ride bikes, the blocks and guys
must be returned to their places. This system is based
less on authoritarian enforcement and more on an
expectation established through natural consequences.
If you dump things where they don't belong, you can't
find something when you want it. If you leave a toy
tornado in the living room, there is no space to play, no
clean slate for the next vignette.

Family responsibility is about the cleaning contributions
we all make to the household and one another.

Something about chore charts makes me want to lash out irrationally (they feel so authoritarian), so I set up a chart, similar to the Weekly Plans we utilize for homeschooling, that is based on choice. There is a list of cleaning chores that need to be completed to keep the house livable. Each child writes his name next to one chore of his choosing each day. Some days they will feel especially motivated and complete a week's worth of chores in one morning while belting along with some rockin' music, then enjoy a cleaning hiatus. The key to having a successful chore system is that it be based on family responsibility, meaning it is not something handed down from the parent level to the child level, but communal in nature. When the children are cleaning up, I join in. When I am cleaning, they are happy to help. There is no external reward, no financial bribe, and no threat of punishment. They have a sense that we are working together for one another.

Schooling Materials

Each child has his own cubby on the shelf containing his curricula. One cubby houses sorted lined, white, and construction paper. Supplies, such as pencils and markers, are organized in a drawer tower under the desk. Their laptop sits atop the desk. The iPad charges in a magazine holder. The printer lives on top of the cubby shelf. A magnetic white board (which displays each child's Weekly Plan) hangs upon the wall. A world map[6] adorns the largest wall. All of the materials that are essential to our more structured learning are woven through what I refer to as our "playroom" (which is open to the living room and the backyard). Keeping all of these materials at their fingertips facilitates their frequent and easy use.

Outdoor Space

Hands down, my favorite part of our house is the backyard. It may not be perfectly manicured, but it hosts daily adventures. This landscape opens the door to an entirely fresh (and healthy) learning and living environment. No matter what form, size, or shape the outdoor space you have access to, take full advantage of it. If you have no outdoor space on your property but frequent a local park, have easily transportable bins with various outdoor materials and activities that you rotate bringing along. If you do have a backyard, set up opportunities for exploration and different aspects of play outdoors just as you do indoors. Studies such as entomology and gardening naturally take root outside. We are currently loving a water station we created to explore the water cycle. My three boys worship the trampoline for exercising spurts of physical energy and thoroughly enjoy the relaxing tranquility of workbooks completed in the hammock. Our next project is to create a sound garden.

Supplies

There are some toys, activities, and supplies we love having at our disposal. You don't need to own everything on this list, but if you want to get started stocking a stimulating playscape, this list of our favorites is a good inspiration to start.

Art

- Dry Erase
- Chalk
- Paint
- Stamps
- Crayons
- Stickers
- Markers
- Colored Pencils
- Scissors
- Tape
- Hole Punch
- Stapler
- Glue
- Clipboard
- Ruler
- Alphabet Flashcards
- Miscellaneous Craft Supplies (string, beads, cotton balls, etc.)

Games:

- The World
- Uno
- Animalogic
- Mancala

Activities

- The Human Body (any anatomy play set)
- Marbles
- Felt Board
- Smart Links
- Magnet Blocks (Tegu)
- Geo Boards
- Counting Dinosaurs
- Unifix Cubes
- Legos
- Large Wooden
- Building Blocks
- Magnetic Tangrams
- Magna Tiles
- Cars
- Music (drums, xylophone, maracas, recorders, kazoos, triangle, etc.)
- Puzzles
- Thomas Trains
- Geo Tracks
- Scale

Pretend Play

- Puppets
- Dress Up (simply save your Halloween costumes each year and add things like super hero capes and a Santa hat)
- Pretend Food
- Pretend Dishes
- Pretend Kitchen (ours is plastic and lives outside)

- Cash Register
- Animals
- Dinosaurs
- Doll House
- Guy Sets (sets of your child's favorite characters)
- Squinkies
- Stacking Dolls

Outdoors

- Trampoline
- Hammock
- Chalk
- Paintbrushes
- Slide
- Chairs
- Water (hose)
- Play-Doh
- PVC Pipes (for water, cars, balls, etc.)
- Sound Garden (wind chimes, pots for banging, etc.)

- Balls
- Plants
- Fruit Trees
- Vegetable Garden
- Small Table with
- Power Wheels
- Kiddie Pool (can be used for water, sand, or as a sensory bin)
- Bike
- Scooter

Sensory Bins

You can use a large, low-profile plastic bin, a small kiddie pool, or even your bathtub for these fun sensory experiences. My son's favorite way to learn to write new words is with his finger, in shaving cream, on a cookie sheet.

- Water Beads
- Moon Sand
- Sno Wonder
- Magnets
- Sea Shells (in sand)
- Special Rocks and Gems
- Ice Water
- Shaving Cream
- Bubbles
- Rice
- Feathers

Sensory Bin: Water Beads

Books

You can visit my blog[7] for an expansive list of children's book reviews but these are a few of our favorites.

- My Many Colored Days by Dr. Seuss
- The Pout-Pout Fish by Deborah Diesen
- I Love You Through and Through by Bernadette Rosetti-Shustak
- Wherever You Are, My Love Will Find You by

Nancy Tillman
- The Dark, Dark Night by M. Christina Butler
- Bear Feels Sick by Karma Wilson
- Relax Kids by Marneta Viegas
- Born with a Bang: The Universe Tells Our Cosmic Story by Jennifer Morgan
- The Lorax, Yertle the Turtle, and The Sneetches by Dr. Seuss
- The Magic Treehouse by Mary Pope Osborne
- Peter and the Starcatchers by Dave Barry and Ridley Pearson
- Harry Potter Series by J.K. Rowling

Integrating your child and his education into your home doesn't mean your house needs to be overrun with primary colors and characters. You can have a stylish space that reflects the dignity of where you are in your life while honoring your child and his valued place in the family. A safe and thoughtful space that considers your parenting priorities enhances connection and leads to a harmonious life. This is your nest. This is where you will spend hours lost in love with your child and forge the memories of your child's milestones. Forget what you thought parenting would look like, and create what brings the most warmth and peace to your family.

If a homeschooling life based on child-led play and discovery is your goal, then the design of your playscape is invaluable. Peruse my Sage Parenting Pinterest page for loads of ideas and inspiration.[15] A space that is calm yet encouraging presents tools for play, discovery, and study in a way that is seamlessly woven into home life.

Gear for Walking the Trail

One key to successfully homeschooling your children is to get to know their unique learning styles (just as becoming an expert on your baby is essential for helping your infant to thrive). How does your child learn best? For example, one of my kids learns through conversation. At the end of his independent work, he always skips over to discuss everything he has just learned. That is how he synthesizes the information. Curricula that revolve around discussion or verbal instruction are ideal for him. Furthermore, a late-morning/mid-day study period is when his brain is most piqued. My other son is repelled by verbal instruction. You could try to explain aeronautical engineering and you would be met with a dismissive, "I know, I know." Don't get me wrong – he is a good listener in general, but the path from "out here" to "in there" (his head) is not through his ears. He is a doer. He learns through hands-on, putting-pencil-to-paper learning. He loves to independently draw and write, so lessons that utilize his hands and fine motor skills are ideal for him. The process of figuring things out on his own is what motivates his learning. To illustrate this concept, my one child learned to read from us reading aloud to each other. My other child learned to read from writing the alphabet and words. Different styles, different strategies, same results.

There is a whole world of curricula out there I didn't even know existed! Did you know that there are a million different ways to learn the same thing?! Whatever your child's strengths, challenges, styles, preferences – there is a curriculum that is a good fit for him. Getting the right curricula for each child has actually been really fun. I research options by looking through the curriculum websites through which our school orders the materials. It's like perusing a catalog of Christmas toys! I read reviews anywhere from Amazon to personal blogs. I ask my homeschooling friends. I post questions on homeschooling social media groups. Once selected, I email our EF, who places the order. Receiving a package of curricula is more exciting than cracking open a box of brand new shoes. Oh the potential!

I would say that my biggest hurdle (if you are religious, I would advise skipping this paragraph) has been weeding out the religion-based programs and materials (since a large portion of homeschooling originated in the religious community). Unfortunately, they aren't stamped with a "Two thumbs up from Jesus!", so you have to really look closely. The two biggest subjects of caution are science (or censored lack thereof) and history (both in an ethnocentric presentation and in the representation of fiction as fact).

We are currently digging ABC Mouse.com, Balance Benders, Dance Mat Typing, Explode the Code, Handwriting Without Tears, Khan Academy, Michael Clay Thomas (MCT), Science Detective, Singapore Math, and Story of the World. We have our staples of journaling and daily reading. Plus we have some other curricula that we use less regularly such as ScienceSaurus, WriteSource, and a few standard science and social studies textbooks. As my boys are still only in third grade and kindergarten, we discover new curricula as new developmental stages and interests erupt, and I encourage you to visit my blog[8] to view an updated list of curricula we love.

In addition to these more comprehensive curricula, we have auxiliary learning options that they also have to choose from, such as certain educational websites on the computer. On the laptop, each child has his own user profile. Within each profile there are bookmarked sites geared just for that child. My 8-year-old likes ABC Ya, Dance Mat Typing, Disney, DIY, Duolingo, Eco Kids, Fold N Fly, Fun Brain, Nasa Kids Club, National Geographic, Khan Academy, Make Me Genius, PBS Go, Pottermore, Spelling City, Starfall, and Wonderopolis. Additionally, my 5-year-old likes ABC Mouse, Curiosityville, Disney Junior, Magic Tree House, and PBS Kids. New sites are created every day, so check my blog[7] for an evolving list and keep an eye out for new creative and fun online learning.

The iPad is one of our favorite educational tools. We can easily take it anywhere (I recommend a screen protector and a Gripcase), and with it a child can interact in a fun, educational, and entertaining virtual environment anywhere from the waiting room of a doctor's office to a restaurant while awaiting the food. I will say that parents can very easily abuse this technology. I wouldn't trade the innovative, self-directed entertainment or conversations shared with my children in these types of settings pre-iPad for anything. Boredom can yield much in the way of invention and calm. But when we're in an 8x8 germ-filled room with a sick baby, waiting three hours for (insert snarky tone) the almighty pediatrician to grace us with her presence (though admittedly, we are exceedingly rarely in need of medical care since switching to homeschooling), the iPad can be sanity saving for everyone. Plus, it really just provides one other option – one additional modality – for tapping into the wealth of information at their fingertips with the Internet. Curious how paper is made? No need to wait for the information to be taught to you by an adult from a scheduled textbook lesson. Drive, responsibility, and authority over their learning are fostered when they can easily pick up an iPad (or other tablet) and educate themselves. A simple Google search and you have a YouTube video, a paper company's website, and educational diagrams explaining the process. Some of their favorite apps are ABC Mouse, ABC Wildlife, Bill Nye the Science Guy, Bubble Math, Captain Squiddy, Cut the Rope, Deep Sea Duel, Dinorama, Dish, Duolingo, Endless ABC, Human Body, Kindle, Little Writer, Marble Math, Math Bingo, Motion Math: Hungry Fish, Mystery Math Town, Netflix, Nova Elements, PBS Kids, Photo Booth, Pick-a-Path, Spelling City, Splash Math, Telling Time, TurtleTrek, Where's My Water/Mickey, Word Bingo, and YouTube. We discover new great apps all the time. Literally every day fantastic new apps are developed, so again, check my blog[7] and surf the app store.

It's about respect through choice. Each child is included in the discussion and decision-making process of choosing a curriculum. Each child is offered a shelf of curriculum options that he can pull from each homeschool day. They are free to select whatever topic within a book that piques their interest today. Our daily routine is designed around the natural rhythms of our children. A variety of modalities are included in the learning options from destinations to workbooks, toys to technology.

Activities extending beyond the pages of a core curriculum or your home environment, traditionally deemed extracurriculars, are also presented as options for a well-rounded development. Each child is allowed to commit to one paid activity at a time that we put on the regular family schedule. My kids are quite enamored with swim, which in addition to satisfying our PE requirement (and is therefore funded through our EUs), is great exercise, teaches a vital safety skill here in San Diego, and provides good socialization. Another favorite of my son's is musical theater. He has been pining to take guitar lessons, so I am currently looking into that. We have done yoga, self-defense, and soccer. We encourage them to try a variety of things to find their passions while requiring that they follow through with the one session to which they committed. Extracurricular activities are offered in every community, so enrich your child with things beyond math and reading. Allow them to try a wide variety of activities of their choosing to really empower them with experiences that spark their interest and motivation.

One word of caution with extracurriculars: they can be overdone. Sometimes in our zealousness to enrich our children with every possible opportunity, we overschedule them. Also take care to grant your children a say in what activities they will devote their time and energy to. You may have loved piano, but your son is not you. You may have had hopes of having a baseball star, while your daughter's passion lies in art. Respect your child's individuality and cheer him on as he goes through the process of discovering himself.

In addition to structured extracurriculars, we also take advantage of our many community resources. This can be free events or places, like concerts in the park or historic reenactments, or paid admission attractions around your town. Passes. We have passes everywhere. In lieu of a pile of more plastic toys your kids don't need or want, ask Grandma and Grandpa to give their beloveds a pass to a community resource they can enjoy all year long. Plus, now gone are the weekends spent fighting crowds. When you go to these places during the week, when the vast majority of the local kid population is in school, the treks are easy and relaxing. We have passes to the Natural History Museum, the Science Center, the Safari Park, the Zoo, the Botanic Garden, etc. My son read about Egypt (the uniting of Upper and Lower Egypt in the early human civilizations), so we headed on over to the Museum of Man and saw a real Egyptian mummy! That is an experience he will not soon forget, and it is only one example of hundreds of times we have been able to take advantage of community resources like that to profoundly impact their learning. Yesterday, at the Safari Park on a playdate with friends, a zoologist asked, "Do you homeschool your kids?" After I responded with a yes, she said, "I can always tell - they are so inquisitive!" Our kids were checking out the animals in their habitats, asking questions, discussing amongst each other, and drawing and writing interesting facts about the animals in their animal journals, all while jumping and playing.

One of the most valuable public resources for most homeschoolers is the library. Any topic of study can be fleshed out with a fun trip to the library and the checking out of a hefty stack of books (even videos). When we lived near a library, we used to ride bikes there often. I had to limit each child to "only" 10 books of their choosing that I would tow back in the bike trailer with my youngest. The library can serve to keep your literary landscape fresh and provide the in-depth information on any topic of interest that can really elevate learning – all for free. Additionally, most libraries offer free classes such as yoga or sign language (and have one amnesty day a month when you can turn in any materials without a late fee).

You may also want to look into any educator discount programs in your community. Teachers enjoy discounts at many places of which homeschool educators also get to take advantage. For example, Barnes and Noble has a teacher discount with which you get 25% off educational items and 25% off everything certain weeks during the year. As with a military or senior discount, you need only ask, and you may uncover an unpublicized discount that can be helpful on your homeschooling journey.

Community resources aren't just places, they are also *people.* Forming a mama tribe is so healthy in creating a community of support for your family. People often wonder how they will make family friends while homeschooling without the forced proximity of traditional school. Getting out there in the world in all the ways I have described keeps you in contact with a variety of people who share similar passions. For example, we found a great Meetup group for "Cool Homeschoolers" that holds meetups all around the county, every single day. I am also a member of a couple Facebook groups based on similar parenting practices. Chatting up the parents of the children whose company your children enjoy at extracurricular activities is always a promising endeavor (and an enjoyable way of passing your time on the sidelines). I have found that the community of people we now enjoy is so much more supportive and authentic than the people we were surrounded by based on nothing more than our classroom placement. Many of the relationships in our lives while in traditional school existed because we had to make the best of the people around us. The relationships we now enjoy are completely by choice, and because of that, we actively invest in each other. Some of our friendships revolve around my children's oldest and dearest friends; family relationships we have cultivated from the early days of baby play groups or carried over from traditional school. Some of our friendships have sprouted from online introductions or our homeschool adventures. We maintain a dynamic tribe of families who help our whole family to be our best selves.

Nature is one of the most valuable of all the educational resources at your disposal (second only to Socratic conversation and followed by the Internet, which puts the world's wealth of knowledge at your child's fingertips). Entire books have been written about the benefits of unstructured time in nature, and I encourage you to give them a look and seriously integrate nature into the life of your child. We are so fortunate to live here in San Diego where we have beaches, inland, mountains, and deserts. But wherever you are, there is nature to be enjoyed. Nature journaling is a favorite of ours. Open your eyes to the fact that nature is a school in and of itself, and you will gain a tremendous asset to your homeschooling life.

Raising
Trailblazers

Now that you're imagining a longhaired boy meditating on life's great mysteries under the shade of a tree (in all fairness, my boys do presently have long hair), I will address a commonly held concern surrounding homeschooling: socialization. For some strange reason, people seem to think that school is the only place socialization takes place. I'll admit I was even worried about being able to meet my son's social needs (as he is such a social butterfly) when first contemplating homeschool. I thought that since he socializes at school all day, removing the school component would remove the socialization. But that is not the way it works. He learns at school all day, but removing school does not mean he will no longer learn anything. The same is true for socialization. When you remove school, something takes its place: real world interaction. There is not just an absence; a whole, beautiful life fills in the space.

I would argue that children who are homeschooled are far more socialized than their traditionally schooled counterparts. You see, homeschooled children exist full-time in a social world that consists of a wide variety of people and settings. They guide those younger, they assist and learn from those older, they read and navigate the appropriate social cues for every completely different activity and place throughout their days. And they transition between these settings and relationships seamlessly. The consequences of social acuity are real for a child living in the real world. Punishments are not manufactured. Social dynamics are not institutionalized and manipulated. If you're a selfish jerk, that other kid is not going to play with you. If you are an empathetic and fun friend, children will gravitate toward creating lasting bonds with you. The feedback is sincere.

The qualities of a successful traditional student are not the qualities of a successful person in today's real world. Think about it. What qualities might constitute a successful classroom student (from the teacher's perspective, as he or she is the judge): silence, unquestioning, obedience, stillness, mediocrity and contentedness to repeat the mundane and ineffective? What qualities result in a successful social position in a traditional school setting: selfishness, cruelty, insincerity, submission, and an overriding willingness to sacrifice individuality to fit in? Now, what qualities will result in a successful person in the society of tomorrow: innovation, creativity, passion, confidence, and outspokenness? My children are remarkably socially competent in the world of playground politics. That's just not the social life I want for them. I happen to be an extrovert who thrives in high-pressure social situations. The qualities within me that allow me to excel socially are *not* the qualities I developed from traditional schooling. The children around me who clawed their way to the top of the traditional school's social hierarchy were nothing like me. Most importantly, they are not the peers of mine who are successful today! What qualities do you want to foster in your child? Are your educational (and parenting, for that matter) choices going to get him there?

Homeschooling fosters responsibility and autonomy. Parents, whose children are coming from the restrictive environment of traditional education where topics and modalities beyond their control are force-fed to them, are often insistent that their children would not be motivated to do anything in their home environment. I assure you that this is not the case. Children are natural-born learners – you just have to get out of their way. By that I mean, be present as a docent to the well of knowledge that is the universe, while allowing them to lead. When you first make the leap, you might find that there is an initial period of lethargy. But that doesn't last long, and once your children realize that this is not a temporary state but a new lifestyle, they settle in and find their equilibrium.

We can insulate our children from a great deal of natural, life learning with an easily spoken but stiflingly restrictive "no." Exploration, experience, autonomy, and *risk* bring awareness. They teach your children firsthand about themselves and the world around them. If you find yourself all too often blurting out or implementing negative and unnecessary limits (think over-babyproofing or reflexive, automatic "nos"), acknowledge that your child's way is not the wrong way while yours is right. This is his journey and you need to let go of your control over some of it. With the requirements of traditional schooling absent, you don't have to control every minute of your child's time or fear self-expression as you might once have. Turn over a new leaf by employing more of *saying nothing* in these situations. Try to flip things to the positive as often as possible ("no yelling" becomes "quiet voices inside, yelling outside"). You want to find a way to say yes, to grant your child as many learning experiences as they are brave enough to take on. Take a step back and be available when asked for help while giving them the lead.

"Can I climb that big rock?!"

"Why might I be worried if you do?"

"Because I could fall down and get hurt."

"Ah, true, true. Why might I say yes?"

"Because it would be good exercise for my muscles and balance."

"Oh, that is a good point; I agree. So what could we do?"

"You could stand right behind me in case I fall. You could hold my hand once I am on the top if I feel unstable."

"That sounds great! Let's do it!"

The 2-year-old version (which took place immediately following his big brother's successful rock adventure):

"You want to jump to that big rock? It's very high. What might happen?"

"Bonka head (hits his head with his hand). Hold it hand (holds out his hand)?"

"That's a safe choice. Ready, set, jump!"

When my West started walking, he lumbered into the great outdoors with a glint in his eye (and we affectionately referred to him as "Tarzan Baby"). We gave him free reign of our large backyard while some of his toddler counterparts were pent up in a playpen or behind a baby gate. At 2, he now has exceptional motor skills and body awareness. While other 2-year-olds are stumbling off curbs, he is able to appropriately assess risks and judge preferred precautions such that he can scale rocky mountains and navigate urban jungles successfully. Has he ever been hurt? Sure! And neither he nor I would trade that invaluable experience for a clean knee.

Part of the true beauty of homeschooling is that life and the universe become your classroom. You are completely free to follow any spark of interest and curiosity and chase it all the way to its natural end. A question about a limpet could go from a children's book to the Internet, to the aquarium, to the tide pools, to emailing with a real-life scientist studying these animals in the professional world. The array of subjects covered by facilitating your child's journey of exploration is truly amazing. It's about learning through the *wonder* of experience.

The curricula provide us a good safety net by filling in any gaps between our practically acquired knowledge (like the math skills required to sort, count, and deposit all of the change in their dino banks at the bank) and knowledge that is necessary for a progressive society, informed democratic electorate, and for my children to have every advantage in finding their passions and reaching their potential (like knowing that a certain type of government attempted in early recorded history resulted in a particular problem for that society).

I view the curricula like the skeleton of my kids' education while our real life experiences contextualize and make relevant (and lasting) new knowledge. Some people opt to forgo the skeletal curricula in favor of unschooling. Unschooling is just as it sounds: You learn from living life, and as new, recognized gaps in your knowledge arise, you learn what you need to fill them in.

My concern for my children with straight unschooling is that I don't believe everything that would be advantageous for them to know would come up in daily life. However, one great lesson I have learned from the unschooling movement (and appreciate) is that your child's education is not a competition. It is not a race. And there is not only one (boring) way to learn something. *There are many paths to wisdom.* The tenets of unschooling have helped me to embrace an educational philosophy that respects each individual child's learning journey and have also helped remind me to trust in my child. He will learn that. It doesn't have to be today, because a schedule told him so. It doesn't have to be from this copied piece of paper. Expand your horizons and let the learning happen more organically. So while true unschooling is not a good fit for our family (I think the Wild Thornberrys rocked it), I am grateful for its valuable lessons. *Learning through living is our primary directive.*

Life on the Trail

The soul-rocking, simple revelation of homeschooling is that it is a lifestyle. You create the life you want for your family. It's really that simple. *Life becomes their full-time job and learning happens within it.* And it isn't just a life you create for your children. You get to realize your own happiness in designing your homeschooling life.

Attachment Parenting (AP) is the style of parenting we have embraced in raising our children from the first moments of their existence. It is an intuitive philosophy in which you base your parenting choices on respecting your child's natural needs and enhancing the bond you share. Homeschooling is a perfect extension of this approach to raising heart-full children that we can now easily carry over throughout our entire lives. We have the power and freedom to meet each child's ever-changing needs on his journey toward becoming his best self. Compassion, empathy, love, fulfillment, respect, growth, connection, and passion are all woven through the overarching curriculum of our daily lives.

The term "homeschooling" is the most widely understood label to communicate our educational approach, though the term doesn't quite sit right with me, just as the label "stay-at-home mom" is one I have never been willing to wear. It doesn't reflect the way in which we live or the way in which we learn. I don't stay at home and we don't strictly learn within the confines of our house. I refer to myself as a full-time mom, as I devote the primary focus of my time and energy to raising my children. I would love a label that more accurately reflects our iteration of the homeschooling lifestyle, but I haven't quite found one that resonates yet. Thirteen-year-old Logan LaPlante has a fantastic video[9] describing his family's approach they call "Hackschooling." Life schooling? Family schooling? World schooling? I'm open to inspiration. For now, the term that most resonates is simply: *life*.

Some families trot the globe and refer to themselves as travelschoolers. Without the geographical and schedule boundaries of traditional school, the world really is your oyster. You can travel and provide your child with exceptionally rich life learning experiences. In all honesty, travel has been outside of our budget and nesting focus in our present phase of life, but we sincerely look forward to taking advantage of all of the physical and cultural wonder this planet has to offer.

Homeschooling can free you to live a family-integrated life. In society today there are so many arbitrary boundaries that serve to artificially compartmentalize our time and internal selves. This is your relationship with your husband. Here is your work life. There is your child. They exist as completely separate entities. Each setting is assumed to be mutually exclusive to any "other" realm of your personhood. This is a huge mistake of our culture. It does not serve us. It does not serve children. It does not serve society. Though you may sometimes find that you are forging an unfamiliar path, homeschooling helps to facilitate this shift. For example, I frequently teach classes with a child under wing. My child benefits from this unique and valuable experience, I am fulfilled in meeting my professional potential, and the families in my classes benefit from the wisdom I have to impart. Win-win-win for all.

Another shift that my younger children benefit from is that their early childhoods are no longer about preparing them to be successful in the traditional school environment. If I had a dollar for every time I heard parents justify a course of premature, forced independence that was not in their child's best interest with, "Well, she needs to learn how to be without a parent, be independent, fight her way to the top, stand up for herself, etc.", then I could afford to fund the dissemination of the substantial body of research illustrating that *independence is not taught, it blooms* directly into their heads. My children's early childhoods are no longer about preparing them to be tossed into the deep end of an environment that does not naturally bring out the best in a young child. We are now free to be *present* without fear of an impending, uncertain future. Decisions for our 2-year-old can be about doing exactly what is right for a 2-year-old, not about preparing him for school survival.

My life while my son was in traditional school was fine, even good. It was as it was "supposed" to be (Another red flag! If you're doing something because you're "supposed to," reevaluate and make a conscious choice!). Being a full-time parent to a child in traditional school felt like work. I was less than fulfilled, doing all the grunt work, giving away the best parts of him, and quite frankly, tasking my time with menial chores. It was an accepted part of life that he would whine, cry, and resist every school morning. He would come home shell-shocked only to have the taste of freedom snatched away by hours of homework. Our lives consisted entirely of transitions: wake up early, get dressed, brush teeth, fix hair, pack lunch, pack backpack, eat breakfast, get in car, drive to school, park, walk to line-up, go to class (insert his day full of regimented "go here, sit down, be quiet"), drive to pick-up an hour before school to get a parking spot, park, walk to gate, drag kids through the crowd back to the car, drive home, wash hands, put away shoes, unpack backpack, eat a snack, cajole him through three hours of homework (On a related note, did you know that research shows absolutely *no* benefit to homework in the elementary years? Alfie Kohn has some superb writing on this subject.), eat dinner, take shower, put on pajamas, brush teeth, brush hair, read book, go to sleep (which had to be enforced because we had to be up so damn early). This was our life. This was it. I have to say, I didn't even realize this was the case until we made the switch, and suddenly our lives were about our lives again. Life became not good, but great. It's like we could breathe again. The vacuum of space created by the absence of transitions was filled with *joy*.

One amazing revelation in our lifestyle change was that homeschooling occupies *less* of my time than traditional schooling. All that time and energy that was sucked away by transitions and fruitless tasks was reclaimed. And the time dedicated to cuddling together and learning about volcanoes, data analysis, and poetic iambs does not feel like a waste. I would not enjoy being a public school teacher (a very noble job that I respect greatly), but I love teaching my children. The role of parent is not diminished to chauffeur. *This feels like the natural state of "parent."* And it feels amazingly fulfilling. I am no longer at the mercy of the real force that was running our lives: the school. My success as a parent is no longer judged by how many tardies are on my child's report card. We no longer have to spend our lives doing what we are "supposed to." We get to do what is best for our kids. We get to do what makes us happy. We get to spend our time doing what we want. That time is now spent engaging with my children in the world, which is great for my kids but also fun for me!

We now get the best of each other. I was taking my son's prime time of day and giving away his best to a setting that didn't appreciate it. No more. We are now free to live by the routine of our natural rhythms. We sleep when we are tired, wake when we are rested, learn when we are most alert, eat when we are hungry, run when we are spirited, and hug when we need it.

In addition to my relationship with my children, their sense of self, their relationship with society and the world around them, and my personal sense of self-flourishing, the relationships between my three boys (which were always wonderful and my greatest reward as a parent to see) are now profoundly deep. You see, this amazing thing just happens when you have multiple children of different ages: They teach each other. Just as they cared for each other and entertained each other, they now teach each other. They have extended that same dynamic into the realm of education, which is wonderful in and of itself. But the profound piece comes in when they realize that they are no longer part-time brothers. They are not devoted to another world of children, leaving their siblings with whatever of them is left over. They are full-time brothers now. I look forward, with great appreciation, to their connected futures.

Looking to the future, the opportunity for our children to attend college is important to my husband and me. We learned so much about the world and ourselves during our time in college. My experience in the world of higher learning truly helped me to realize a lot of my potential. That said, I would never pressure my children with college mandates. But I would also never do anything that would potentially close any doors for them. Thankfully, the facts don't lie, and homeschoolers are graduating high school and attending college at higher rates than traditional students and earning better

GPAs once there.

Don't Step in the Poison Oak

While this is all great news, and rainbows and butterflies have been bursting off the pages, there are some not-so-glorious aspects to the homeschooling lifestyle that are mostly practical and obvious in nature.

Sometimes, my kids don't want to do their work. Part of what makes homeschooling so wonderful is that we have the ability to change the setting or choose a different subject. This, along with some attention, is usually enough to right the ship. However, I am careful to balance taking advantage of the child-directed and flexible nature of homeschool learning with not setting a precedent of, "If you protest, then you don't have to do it." I have found that this dynamic is the same one that plays out in myriad scopes of our lives. My son doesn't want to take the recycle out today (his chore), so I remind him that we all have to help and work together to keep the house a nice place to live. That said, I tell him I would be happy to take out the big trash now so we can walk out together. This is simply another example of how education is incorporated into everyday life and parenting in general.

One caregiver must be present with the children. Homeschooling does not necessarily require a stay-at-home parent, but it does sacrifice the free childcare that traditional school provides for a dual-income family. As most of the homeschooling families I personally know have higher degrees (including my husband and I) (teachers, therapists, psychologists, doctors, scientists, lawyers, entrepreneurs, etc.), professional careers and a homeschooling lifestyle are not mutually exclusive. But it does certainly require flexibility and creativity that not every parent is in a position to employ. Some co-parents work differing schedules and equally split the homeschooling and parenting (though, as I have explained, there is not really a distinction between the two realms). Some families have an extended family member who cares for their children during their working hours. In today's professional climate, many homeschooling parents are able to work from home some or all of the time. In addition to being a full-time homeschooling parent, I also run a company called Sage Parenting[10], through which I write (Captain Obvious), teach, coach, and speak. My husband works full-time, sometimes outside of the home, sometimes telecommuting from home. We are also blessed with (and grateful for) the support of my parents, who are involved and available.

Since you will now be the one raising your children (not strangers and not a large group of their peers), you will be spending a lot of time with them.

I happen to like my children; it's why I decided to have them. But I recognize that not everyone is their best self, spending all of their time with their children. It can be a challenge to maintain your sanity if you spend every waking moment knee-deep in ABCs and sticky hands. But I would argue that much of the condition of parents not wanting to parent their children full-time is more a symptom of a grossly non-child/parent-friendly society. Parents can easily become isolated in the limited parts of society deemed "child-friendly," cut off from the things in life that bring stimulation and joy to Mom and/or Dad (not to mention by financial pressures). In an ideal world (and I strive to live the change I want to see), parents wouldn't have to choose between a Chuck E. Cheese's life sentence and a courtroom career. Living a family-integrated lifestyle means everyone is fulfilled, and we are all better for it.

Your children are also spending the bulk of their time together.
This can be a great asset, as I have discussed. Sibling relationships that are carefully cultivated and nurtured will be powerfully positive, lifelong forces in each child's life. They also have the potential to be torturous. I have an important chapter on siblings in my book *Sage Parenting: Where Nature Meets Nurture*[11] with the formula for raising siblings successfully. Suffice it to say, really doing your homework and investing in this arena will yield great dividends.

If you are co-parenting, be sure that the domestic and childrearing responsibilities are equally shared.
Some question what that looks like. In my family, I am a full-time parent, not a housewife. This means that the domestic responsibilities are not mine alone. The household chores are divided evenly (e.g., my husband does dishes, I do laundry). Every minute that he is home, he is fully engaged in 50% of the parenting responsibility. We make a financial sacrifice so that I can dedicate my time, energy, and attention to raising our

young children, not to cleaning the house.

Also be sure to have some things in your life that feed
your sense of being outside parenthood.
I have my work, which is engaging and rewarding. At
least one of my children is usually with me while I am
working, and I love that. I don't require physical distance
from them to nurture the other parts of me. I also do
Krav Maga[12], which is great exercise and empowering
to boot. I have my relationship with my husband, whom
I absolutely adore. We are co-parents, but we also have
a fun relationship that underlies that role. I also have my
friends, whom I sincerely enjoy hanging out with as our
children play. Sometimes, I get just as much out of the
playdates as my children.

Making connections requires more effort.
I have discussed the many ways you can forge
friendships to form a quality community of
homeschooling peers. Yet the fact does remain that
you must actually reach out to make those connections.
This can take time and persistence, but don't become
discouraged. Just because peers and activities (and
learning) aren't force-fed to you and your child as they
might be in traditional school, that doesn't mean they
can't be abundant in your life. Keep your head up and
your eyes and arms open, and people of similar passions
will be drawn to you. When you live authentically and
confidently, keeping your compass set to your child's
best interest, there is a gravitational force that attracts
others with whom you all can share your homeschooling
journey.

Lastly, don't become trapped and isolated in your house.
Regular connection with the outside world, integrated
into your lifestyle, is beneficial for your children and
healthy for you. It can seem daunting to get the train
moving out the door – trust me, I know. But it is crucial
for their well being and your sanity. When I'm having a
stressful day, I drop everything and we just go. Soak up

that vitamin D from the sun, set your little ones free in nature, and re-center.

10

The Path Less Traveled

One function traditional school does serve that can suffer with completely independent homeschooling is that of a sort of safety net, checking in on children. This is particularly poignant in the case of abused or neglected children for whom the six-hour freedom from parental abuse and mandated reporting by teachers could be lifesaving. In a less severe case, if a child is intentionally isolated by his parent or intentionally misinformed, school can remedy that by offering a degree of diversity and exposure to universal ideas. Of course, all this is also accomplished with a high quality homeschool charter program like ours.

There is one second-order downside to homeschool that impacts society as a whole. I whole-heartedly believe that a country needs public education as an inalienable right. *Humanity benefits when we can all stand on the shoulders of the knowledge established before us and reach higher.* I don't necessarily believe that homeschool is the solution to the problems in the current (and grossly outdated) state of education in this country, but I can't sacrifice my children to try to change it for the better from within. Honestly, I don't have the solution. I am hopeful for other people to come along and actually revolutionize this system that is so stuck, based on our modern, scientifically backed understandings of children and learning. Charter schools are one attempt at circumventing the stagnation of the traditional public education system. I know our homeschool charter school is what is in my child's best interest today, and I have to be loyal to that priority.

One promising, revolutionary concept currently being studied is "flipping the classroom." I first heard of the concept through Khan Academy and it's actually quite brilliant. It involves setting up an educational format in which children learn new concepts on their own at home (with the help of an online system like Khan Academy), and then classroom time is when students practice the concepts they are working through, and the teacher moves freely among students to provide individual assistance. Flipping the classroom in this way would resolve some of the problems we currently experience under the traditional school model. Each student would be free to move at his own pace and in his own self-motivated directions. The classroom would provide the playground, peer group, and teacher feedback to play with and accommodate all the newly acquired concepts. Of course, you still have major downsides such as a total disconnect from real world context in its current iteration. But I can see potential to expand the formula in other exciting ways, and I look forward to seeing the effects of the fruits of this research on the fate of traditional schooling.

Another exciting new concept I have seen in revolutionizing traditional public education is called Modern Learning Environments[13] (MLE). They entail completely ditching the rows of desks with the teacher/lecturer model and replacing them with an environment that respects children as people and is actually conducive to learning in the way that we now understand it to take place in children. These spaces are designed intuitively with components such as reclined reading spaces and a refrigerator for food access.

As someone with a great deal of education under her belt (as my student loan debt can attest to), who values that accomplished knowledge above all other non-living things (as it allows me to help you now), I have prodigious respect for education and teachers. My praise for homeschooling is in no way an indictment of the thousands of teachers who go to work every morning, compensated with a fraction of their value, genuinely trying to make a positive contribution to children. I wouldn't want formal teachers to become extinct in my perfect world. We have a fond appreciation for the role of my sons' learning center teachers and our EF (who are all credentialed teachers). The system just needs to change. Why does it look the way it does? We are no longer grooming assembly line workers in industrial factories. The world has changed. We have (ironically) learned through systematic research that we are approaching this thing wrong. Yet it stands. So I empower you not to settle for what is expected and accepted. Find or create the reality that is in your child's best interest. I may not have all the answers, but I do know that without the shackles of the traditional learning environment, my children are soaring.

The next step in growing into our potential on our homeschooling journey is to expand our minds to attain even more of that core-curriculum-based learning from child-driven passions in the real world. For example, my son devotes a good amount of time and energy to filming and creating videos. I am researching programs that he could learn to use (a valuable tech skill) to elevate the level of videos he can create. He could write tutorials for other children, which he could share online to help others with a similar passion. He is also very excited about learning the ukulele. He is having a lot of fun taking lessons and practicing, and learning the language of musical theory definitely taps into the math centers of the brain. He is a profound champion of social justice, so I would love to find projects he could work on that could help a cause close to his heart. It's about learning through living life and making the world a better place.

11

Mapping your Journey

My intention in writing this book is to provide you with a trail guide to help you intentionally choose the best path for your child and family. My hope would be that you walk away with a sense of respect for your own personal journey, a broader perspective on your child's education, and an understanding of homeschool as an accessible, achievable, and desirable option. I wanted to be sure to dispel some common misconceptions and warn of some potential pitfalls. Most importantly, I wanted to paint a how-to picture of a homeschooling life: a lifestyle of connection in which a child's natural learning can flourish.

If you are ready to explore your own options, the first step is research. You likely have numerous possible options, which can be simultaneously wonderful and daunting. Thoroughly investigate each possibility so you have a clear view of which paths you could take. Then you can make one informed choice.

Start by searching your school district's website, or even give the district a call and ask if they have a homeschool program. Next, I would recommend an online search with your city's name followed by "homeschool" and then "charter school." Make a list of all your local options and resources. After that, search your state's independent homeschool requirements. The search will likely lead you to a state site with a form to fill out and submit to establish yourself as an independent school. Next, a web search for "online homeschool" will display numerous options for all-inclusive, online homeschool programs. Then you really want to tour each local program that you think might be a good fit. A lot can be gleaned from an in-person visit that just cannot be through a website or phone call. Lastly, check out homeschooling groups through social media like Facebook and Meetup. Connecting with like-minded families will start you on your way to building a supportive and encouraging homeschooling community.

Once you are armed with all the options at your disposal, you will be able to start making some decisions. Which education option is the best choice for your child? Cast off your preconceived notions of what "should" be and think only about your individual kid and what environment would most bring out his strengths and help with his challenges. In what setting would this little person thrive? Remember, if you begin walking down a path and it doesn't feel right, you can always go in another direction.

Once your decision is made and your arrangements are set (your child is enrolled), it is time to come out of the homeschooling (if that is your choice) closet. Telling your family and friends about non-traditional choices can be difficult in some communities and families. But as with all aspects of parenting, doing what is best for your child is more important than placating people on the outside looking in. Hope for the best response (support and encouragement), prepare for the worst (criticism and discouragement). Think about how you can respond to their potential reactions in non-defensive ways. "Thank you for your feedback, as I know you care a great deal for me and my child. We have not come to this decision lightly, and we are confident and optimistic in our choice to homeschool." Some close family members, whose support you would greatly appreciate, might express some specific concerns that you could address through resources like this easily digestible infographic, which contains some superb hard data: Homeschool Domination: Why These Kids Will Take You Down.[14]

This worksheet can help to guide your transition into the world of homeschooling by creating your own personal trail map. Laying out and marking your potential paths can aid in the decision-making process, while the questions can serve to launch you into action.

Homeschool Program Options
You will choose only one of these paths for your child, but thoroughly researching all of your options makes for an informed decision.

Local School District
Does your local school district have a homeschool program?
How does the program work?
How often do you meet with a teacher?
Do you have a say in the curriculum?
Do you have access to local school auxiliary programs (such as band)?
Pros/Cons?

Local Homeschool Charters
How does the program work?
What are their philosophies about how children learn?
How often do you meet with a teacher?
Is there an in-person learning center component?
Does the school provide or pay for curriculum materials?
Pros/Cons?

Local Charters
How does the program work?
What are their philosophies about how children learn?
What is the mood of the classroom environment?
What does the parent involvement look like?
In what way is it different from traditional school?
Pros/Cons?

Online Homeschool Programs
How does the program work?
Is there a cost?
What is the workload?
Is there any parent involvement?
Can you individualize the curriculum?
Pros/Cons?

Independent Homeschooling
What are the state requirements?
Where will you seek support/guidance/resources?
Pros/Cons?

Homeschool Resources

Local Homeschool Resources
Are there any local homeschooling social groups?
What local community resources would enhance your
homeschooling?
What extracurricular activities operate in your
community?

Virtual Homeschool Resources
What virtual social homeschooling groups can you join?

What are some quality online curricula retailers?

Playscape Materials
What materials could enhance your child's playscape?
What changes could you make to your child's environment to enhance his learning experience?

Curricula Materials
What curricula would be a good fit for your child?

References

1. Schools Kill Creativity by Sir Ken Robinson: http://www.ted.com/talks/ken_robinson_says_schools_kill_creativity.html
2. Dehesa Charter School: http://www.dehesacharterschool.org/site/default.aspx?PageID=1
3. The Golden Buddha metaphor: http://youtu.be/HCv7-x91G9k
4. Finding Joe by Patrick Takaya Solomon: http://findingjoethemovie.com
5. Modular Latch Box: http://www.walmart.com/ip/Sterilite-2.7-Quart-Latch-Box-Set-of-6/20699631
6. World Wall Map: http://www.ikea.com/us/en/catalog/products/70119430/
7. Children's Books Favorites (with reviews), article on my Sage Parenting blog: http://www.sageparenting.com/childrens-book-favorites/
8. Curriculum Favorites (with reviews) article on my Sage Parenting blog: http://www.sageparenting.com/homeschooling-curriculum-favorites/
9. Hackschooling Makes Me Happy by Logan LaPlante: http://www.collective-evolution.com/2014/01/07/this-is-what-happens-when-a-kid-leaves-traditional-education/
10. Sage Parenting: http://www.sageparenting.com
11. Sage Parenting: Where Nature Meets Nurture: http://www.sageparenting.com/sage-parenting-book/
12. Krav Maga: http://sdcombat.com
13. Modern Learning Environments: http://www.core-ed.org/thought-leadership/white-papers/modern-learning-environments
14. Homeschool Domination: Why These Kids Will Take You Down: http://www.collegeathome.com/

homeschool-domination/

15. Sage Parenting Pinterest Page: http://www.pinter-est.com/sageparenting/

Made in the USA
San Bernardino, CA
29 February 2016